I0018802

Thomas Steen

Automate ASP Core with Roslyn

An alternative way to avoid TT/T4 templates to build controllers, models,

razor views and pages

VERO Verlag

Thomas Steen

Automate ASP Core with Roslyn

An alternative way to avoid TT/T4 templates to build controllers, models, razor views and pages

ISBN/EAN: 9783956107672

Auflage: 1

Erscheinungsjahr: 2019

Erscheinungsort: Norderstedt, Deutschland

VERO Verlag

Automate ASP Core with Roslyn

An alternative way to avoid TT/T4 templates to build
controllers, models, razor views and pages

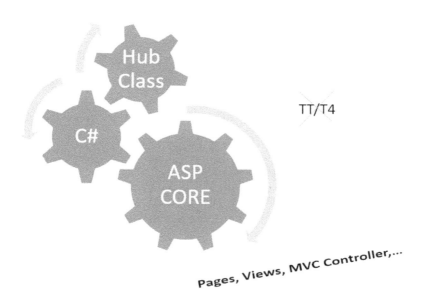

TT/T4

Pages, Views, MVC Controller,...

Thomas Steen

Content

1.   Introduction

Often, we are developing data driven software with 40 to 50 tables. To increase efficiency and reduce costs we used TT Files to automate as much as possible. With the reduced support and the agile changing of the views to pages, regular ASP Core versions updates, Bootstrap updates and so on, this results in the impossibility to deal with these circumstances anymore.

To create early previews for the customer, enhanced with a bunch of standard functions, we don't love doing this by hand. We want to enhance features and do not waste our time for repeating standards.

On the other hand, tools like Roslyn are getting more serious and they are not often used currently to support Model building and creating files.

We want to close the gap and support you to automate the ASP Core with Entity Framework for creating Models, controllers, views and pages. The source code is provided as „as is" and you can change everything you want to fit your own needs. We will explain you detailed what to do. We will use Roslyn to analyze existing Models and create new Models, controllers and classes for pages. For views and the HTML part of pages we cannot use Roslyn. Here we will take advantage of easy to use String Operations to create the appropriate source code. The current created source code focusses on ASP Core 2.2 because during the time of writing this version is the current version. But we checked against ASP MVC on .NET Basis and the Preview of ASP Core 3.0, we can leverage all features and the software can handle these changes well.

This book will shorten your learning curve and you can focus on different interesting programming needs.

Additionally, features we will focus on:

- Import existing C# Models and generate C# Models, controllers, pages and views

- Save created classes for further use

We will write any generated source code in a separate folder structure to avoid conflicts such as overwriting of existing code and projects. Additionally, we will assume that you have already created a project for ASP Core and Entity Framework. We will not focus on creating these parts.

We will focus on the most important data annotations and variable types. If you need more or different one, please add them easily. In the upcoming chapters we will describe the how to do in detail. The created code will follow the code in Microsoft Docs.

We add the Features from Microsoft Docs partly. The explanation in Microsoft Docs is only on a basic level. The provided TT Files doesn't reflect the shown examples in the Docs. But we will give you the opportunity to raise the limits with your own standards. We give you a small web application with only 3 tables showing the implemented features as an example.
https://www.norlinger.com/en/AspAutomateApp/Example

You can reciprocate: "But with reflection we can do everything dynamically." Yes, you are right. But reflection cost CPU Power and in cloud times this cost money and time, avoiding reflection is for us a proper way to save customers money.

Secondary reflection is sometimes not flexible enough. Especially when you want to change small things on one of your views or pages, then you have to break the automatic or dynamic creation. This results in creating the page or view from ground up.

Here we jump in. We create views and pages with full source code, and you can change afterwards everything you want but the base of the view or page looks every time the same.

As always, it's possible to make everything better, nicer, more efficient code, structure the software in a different way and implement different ideas. We appreciate all those thinking, and we love to learn. Our idea is to shorten your learning curve to be more independent from the existing automation environment. Do not hesitate to change everything you want.

We try to find the balance between an expert and an intermediate. If we doesn't meet this, leave us a comment on
https://www.norlinger.com/en/AspAutomateApp/Contact, please.

1.1.   Licenses, liability and trademarks

Trademarks:

The book is related to Microsoft Visual Studio and ASP Core with Entity Framework.

This Book is an independent publication and is neither affiliated with, nor authorized, sponsored or approved by Microsoft Corporation.

As an example of the usage within the book we use "POWERED BY TINY", see details here: https://www.tiny.cloud/.

TinyMCE® is a registered trademark of Tiny Technologies, Inc.

If you have questions, please let us now. Please use the following website https://www.norlinger.com/en/AspAutomateApp/contact. You can send your Feedback anonymous or with your data. If you add your personally data, we will use this only for your question or feedback to your ask.

You can use the provided source code in your environment without any fees. You can change and fit this source code for your own needs.

It's not allowed to distribute this source code to the public.

A big thanks to my wife Carola, she is always believing in me and support generously to achieve this result.

1.2.   Overview of usage

Let us start to describe how you can use this program most efficiently. We have
two starting points:

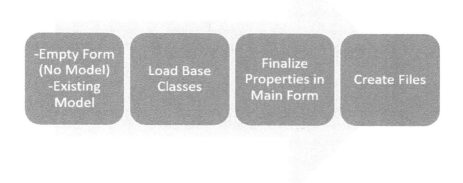

The first starting point is a new ASP Core development and you have no
predefined Model classes. In the main form

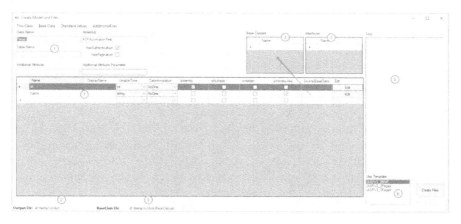

you fill out the fields like class name and so on. For your convenience some fields
of the main form are already filled out. If you want other prefilled values, please
change the return values in the Standards class.

In the property window

you entered all your needed properties of your Model. The header line guides you to the projection in the target class. For a more detailed view on a single property hit the edit button at the end of the line. For your convenience is the key value as an integer already prefilled. If you want to change this standard behavior, please change the values in the Standards class. Additionally, we added the property "Name" because this is often needed. If you want to start with the real clear Main Form, please choose the menu "This Class" and then the menu item "Clear all values". To get the prefilled values again choose the item "Reset all Values".

The second starting point is you have already an existing database schema and you want to rebuild parts or the whole application with the new ASP Core technologies. If you have the Model classes in C# available than you can choose in the menu "This class" the menu item "Import class". All identifiable properties and attributes will be shown in the form. When you use tools like EF Power Tools the full Model class will be created by this tool. Import them as described.

If you want to add, change or remove properties do as you want: the form will behave as a standard windows form.

Let me point out here how to handle base classes of your Model. Please copy all your base classes into the base class directory. The path is shown into the status bar of the form. A double-click on the path will open the Windows Explorer. Keep in mind that the base classes must be loaded into the main form to have them available later to create the views or pages.

If you start your Model from scratch, please enter your base classes in the order of the chain into the base class window. At creation time of the files only the first base class is used.

If you start importing an existing Model class with the hierarchy of base classes than the importing routine will add the base classes to the base class window. If you use EF Power Tools to create the Model classes, the EF Power Tools will not pay attention to the base classes. So, you have to remove all properties, which belong to your base classes and add your base classes manually to the base class list. When you finished adding all your properties choose from the menu "base class" the menu item "Load base classes". All the properties belonging to the base classes will be added automatically and get a filled-out value to which the base class will belong.

When all the properties and values are set correctly choose the template, for example "IASP2_2MVC", and hit the button "Create files". All the files which are created will be stored in the output directory. A double-click on the path of the output directory will start the Windows Explorer.

When you create the Model classes for person and country of origin and connection status your views or pages should look like this following collage:

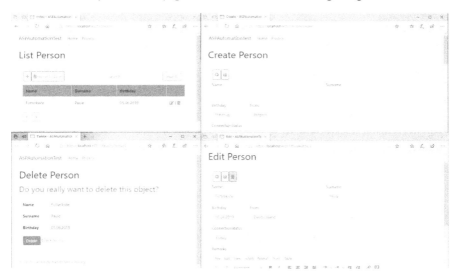

This will end the overview. Later in the book we focus more on the details.

1.3.   Prepare the environment

To run the program, you need a current Windows PC with Visual Studio installed.
There aren`t really dependencies on the versions but do not expect that old
versions are running. We developed and tested everything on Windows 10 and
Visual Studio 2019/2017. As graphical interface we use Windows Forms. From
our perspective the easiest way and understandable for the majority of
developer to build this automation and adopt and integrate this in your own
environment.
If you are running on Mac please choose your graphical interface as needed. The
code is separated from the graphical interface and you can simply build your
frond end.

Please download the source code from
https://www.norlinger.com/en/AspAutomateApp/AppV1. There will be
additional notes and the source code as zip.

We are happy to get your feedback. Please send me a note using the contact
form. (https://www.norlinger.com/en/AspAutomateApp/Contact) You can do
this anonymously or if you want an answer please add your mail address.

To help you starting the program immediately and to get your desired output we
will focus on a few things which you have to fit to your environment.

After you opened the solution within your Visual Studio please go to the helper
folder and open the Standards.cs file. As we said earlier we want to have the
program as much as possible independent from the surface of the tool.

The constructor of the standards class has the most imported settings.

```
public Standards()
{
    OutPutDirectory = @"d:\temp\roslyn";
    BaseClassesDirectory = @"d:\temp\roslyn\BaseClasses";
    NameofStartButton = "Create Files";
    ExtensionPreset = "json";
}
```

The output directory is the path where the program writes all the source files.
You must have the right to create directories and source files. The base classes
directory holds all your base classes. You must copy all your base classes to this
directory. The right to read files is enough. The name of the start button is as
expected, and you can change the text of the start button in the main form. To
easily reload Model classes for further usage you can set the extension. We will

use "json", because it is a json-file, but you can change it if you want. When these settings are done and the new Nuget files are downloaded the solution should work.

Into the solution we added an additional project "ASPAutomationTest" which you can use as a test environment for your created classes.

2.   Roslyn

With the publication of Roslyn a few years ago everybody has the ability to create conform source code. Unfortunately reading and creating source code is not so easy as is looks like. We will show you all needed knowhow to read and write the necessary classes for ASP Core with Entity Framework.

We will use Roslyn in the following ways:

- Reading Model classes (C#), with all needed features like reading properties and attributes
- Writing Model classes (C#) with all needed features like properties, constructor, attributes and extensions for the Model (MVC SelectList)
- Writing the MVC controller class and the page class

Additionally, we will write the MVC controller, views and pages (HTML Part) as string operation. Creating the views and pages could not be done by Roslyn because of the lack of support. The views and pages will be created as strings and then written to disk. The advantage here is that we have the hub class with all features, and we can use the full flavor of our writing environment. Having this in mind we should easier make all the standard stuff for ASP Core with EF.

If you want to use your TT files for the views and pages feel free, it's easy to adopt.

2.1.   Roslyn basics

To understand the following chapter with Roslyn a little bit easier we want to make a small deep dive into the view from a Roslyn perspective into a source code file.

On the left side of the picture you can see the Person Model class and on the right side the syntax view from Roslyn. The used RoslynWrapper hides a few details from your coding and you don´t have to care about these details. But with this knowledge some of the topics will be clearer.

The syntax is organized in a syntax tree where every object is presented as a node.

The compilation unit is the beginning of the tree and the full file which is parsed. The full file is starting at character 0 and goes until character 1585. This is the meaning of [0..1585].

The example you see here is the Person Model file, which we added to the test project and the file is part of the full source code as well. The numbers may vary in the final source code.

The next node after the compilation unit is the using directive. We see from 0..13 the "Using System;". Every using directive node represents the using and the name of the file to use and where the position of this node in the full file is.

After listing all using directives the namespace is placed in the namespace declaration. The namespace has his own keyword and an identifier with his name. When we click on the identifier, we will get "ASPAutomationTest.Models".

A few characters (spaces) later the class declaration will begin. The class declaration has an identifier which is not surprising. In the lower field you can see the identifier and the value is "Person". It's identical to our class name.

In addition, we have all the keywords presented like public, partial and so on. The AttributeList is present so the class will have additional attributes. This is correct because we have the table attribute. When we unfold this, we can see the attribute details.

```
using System;
using System.Collections.Generic;
using System.ComponentModel.DataAnnotations;
using System.ComponentModel.DataAnnotations.Schema;
using System.Threading.Tasks;
using System.Text;
using Microsoft.AspNetCore.Mvc.Rendering;
using System.Linq;
using Microsoft.AspNetCore.Mvc;
using Microsoft.EntityFrameworkCore;
using Microsoft.Extensions.Logging;
using ASPAutomationTest.Models;

namespace ASPAutomationTest.Models
{
    //Model Class
    [Table("Person")]
    public partial class Person
    {
        [Key]
        [HiddenInput]
        [Required]
        public int Id { get; set; }
        public string Name { get; set; }
        public string Surname { get; set; }
        [DataType(DataType.Date)]
        public DateTime Birthday { get; set; }
        [DataType(DataType.MultilineText)]
        public string Remarks { get; set; }
        [Display(Name = "From")]
        public virtual CountryOfOrigin CountryOfOrigin { get; 
        public int CountryOfOriginId { get; set; }
        public virtual ConnectionStatus ConnectionStatus { get;
        public int ConnectionStatusId { get; set; }
        [DataType(DataType.MultilineText)]
        public string ZweiterRemark { get; set; }
    }

    static public partial class PersonExtension
    {
        public static SelectList SelectList(this DbSet<Person>
        {
            SelectList res = new SelectList(dbset.AsNoTracking(
            return res;
        }
    }
}
```

Syntax Visualizer

Syntax Tree

- ▲ NamespaceDeclaration [406..1585]
  - ▷ NamespaceKeyword [406..415]
  - ▷ QualifiedName [416..440]
  - ▷ OpenBraceToken [442..443]
  - ▲ ClassDeclaration [468..1262]
    - ▲ AttributeList [468..485]
      - ▷ OpenBracketToken [468..469]
      - ▲ Attribute [469..484]
        - ▷ IdentifierName [469..474]
        - ▲ AttributeArgumentList [474..484]
          - OpenParenToken [474..475]
          - ▲ AttributeArgument [475..483]
            - ▲ StringLiteralExpression [475..483]
              - StringLiteralToken [475..483]
          - CloseParenToken [483..484]
      - ▷ CloseBracketToken [484..485]
    - ▷ PublicKeyword [491..497]
    - ▷ PartialKeyword [498..505]
    - ▷ ClassKeyword [506..511]
    - ▷ IdentifierToken [512..518]
    - ▷ OpenBraceToken [524..525]
    - ▷ PropertyDeclaration [535..620]
    - ▷ PropertyDeclaration [630..662]
    - ▷ PropertyDeclaration [672..707]
    - ▷ PropertyDeclaration [717..790]
    - ▷ PropertyDeclaration [800..879]

Properties

Type	AttributeSyntax
Kind	Attribute
HasLeadingTrivia	False
HasStructuredTrivia	False
HasTrailingTrivia	False
IsMissing	False
IsStructuredTrivia	False
Language	C#
Name	Table
Parent	[Table("Person")]
RawKind	8848
Span	[469..484]
SpanStart	469

We choose this picture that you can see the parent which results in our expected [Table("Person"]. The attribute himself is the table attribute having some arguments "Person". The attribute himself is surrounded by the bracket token. Later in the chapter when we have to read and write attributes, we must consider that there might be arguments or even not. A property can have arguments as well and it follows the same rules, and here we have to look as well for the attribute arguments.

The rest of the Model class visualizing is straight forward after a list of properties declarations but there can be methods also. The second-class declaration will begin. In this Model file we have a second class with a select list as an extension.

The EndofFileToken is the end of the file.

With this basic knowledge about the construction of the Roslyn parser you should easy understand the next chapter.

To install the syntax visualizer on your own the literature is a subject to change. You must use the Visual Studio Installer (checked with VS 2019) select Change Configuration and select the Single Components Sheet and add these elements.

☑ .NET Compiler Platform SDK
☑ C#- und Visual Basic Roslyn-Compiler

Now you have the extended Syntax Visualizer in your views. Start the view and open a new C#-File. Then you will see the parsed syntax.

2.2.   Parse the Model class (RoslynReadWrapper)

To convert a C# Model class into our hub class we have to identify all the important topics. In this book we will address the most used properties and attributes. It's not a full Roslyn companion, the feature used are reduced and simplified to the need of ASP Developers. If you are missing anything you have the base to add this with a small amount of time.

We build two wrapper classes for Roslyn: one for reading and one for writing. Both classes are static because Roslyn returns always a new created object and so we have no benefits from storing the object.

Let's have a look to a standard Model class, to identify what we want to read from a Model class. The Model class can come from Model creation with the Entity Framework Tools or an old model class from a different project, older versions and so on.

```
namespace ASPAutomationTest.Models
{
    //Model Class
    [Table("Person")]
    public partial class Person
    {
        [Key]
        [HiddenInput]
        [Required]
        public int Id { get; set; }
        public string Name { get; set; }
        public string Surname { get; set; }
        [DataType(DataType.Date)]
        public DateTime Birthday { get; set; }
        [DataType(DataType.MultilineText)]
        public string Remarks { get; set; }
        [Display(Name = "From")]
        public virtual CountryOfOrigin CountryOfOrigin { get; set; }
        public int CountryOfOriginId { get; set; }
        public virtual ConnectionStatus ConnectionStatus { get; set; }
        public int ConnectionStatusId { get; set; }
        [DataType(DataType.MultilineText)]
        public string ZweiterRemark { get; set; }
    }
}
```

We are not interested in all information from the class while reading. The using's and the table name we will ignore. Because we are going to write our new standards during the creation process.

Before we can read, we must create a class node from the C# file content. We will focus only on the first class node because we assume there will be only one class per file.

```
public static ClassDeclarationSyntax GetFirstClassNode(string content)
{
    SyntaxTree tree = CSharpSyntaxTree.ParseText(content);
    SyntaxNode node = tree.GetRoot();
    var classNode = node.DescendantNodes().OfType<ClassDeclarationSyntax>().FirstOrDefault();
    return classNode;
}
```

We are getting all class related information out of the file.

To identify the class, we will hand over the complete C# file as string. Roslyn will parse the content and identify the root. We know that all elements will be held in a list of nodes. Here we are interested in class declaration and we filter the type ClassDeclarationSyntax to get the list of all class declarations and return the first one. Exception checking is for easier reading not shown.

The returned classNode is our central object and from this object we can generate all detailed information.

2.2.1.　　GetName classDeclarationSyntax

The easiest information is the name of the class.

```
public static string GetName(ClassDeclarationSyntax classNode)
{
    return classNode.Identifier.Text;
}
```

The parameter here is our classNode from the beginning of the parsing.

2.2.2.　　GetNameSpace

To get the namespace we have a little bit more to do. You can see in the picture of the model class that the namespace stands above the class declaration. This results that we must go up from our classNode. The classNode held all information of our source code file.

```
public static string GetNameSpace(ClassDeclarationSyntax classNode)
{
    CompilationUnitSyntax cu = classNode.SyntaxTree.GetCompilationUnitRoot();
    MemberDeclarationSyntax firstMember = cu.Members[0];
    NamespaceDeclarationSyntax nsname = (NamespaceDeclarationSyntax)firstMember;
    return nsname.Name.ToFullString().Split('.').First();
}
```

We take the syntax tree and extract the CompilationUnitRoot. This object has the
needed members. As always in Roslyn we must cast the elements to the right
object. After casting we get the needed information.

2.2.3.   GetBaseClasses and interfaces

The function is reading all the base classes and interfaces from our source code.
We assume that the Interfaces started with an 'I' and the base classes not. The
base list of the classNode holds this information.

```
public static IEnumerable<BaseTypeSyntax> GetInterfaces(ClassDeclarationSyntax classNode)
{
    return classNode.BaseList?.Types
        .Where(t => ((IdentifierNameSyntax)t.Type).Identifier.Text[0] == 'I');
}
```

2.2.4.   GetName BaseTypeSyntax

The BaseTypeSyntax has his own routine for the GetName.

```
public static string GetName(BaseTypeSyntax baseType)
{
    return ((IdentifierNameSyntax)baseType.Type).Identifier.Text;
}
```

2.2.5.   GetMembers

All properties are listed in the members list. We return all of them.

```
public static SyntaxList<MemberDeclarationSyntax> GetClassMembers(ClassDeclarationSyntax classitem)
{
    return classitem.Members;
}
```

After we can read all of the class related information we can focus more on the
properties. As we can see in our model class we have a bunch of properties

decorated with several attributes and some attributes with parameters. Not shown in the picture we can have ICollection and navigation properties. For a detailed explanation of these objects please use the Docs.

Additionally we can have functions and constructors.

Our GetMemberlist from the class section returns MemberDeclarationSyntax so our new element to parse is of type MemberDeclarationSyntax.

2.2.6.   Identify the constructor or property

```
public static bool IsConstructor(MemberDeclarationSyntax member)
{
    return member.IsKind(SyntaxKind.ConstructorDeclaration);
}


public static bool IsProperty(MemberDeclarationSyntax member)
{
    return member.IsKind(SyntaxKind.PropertyDeclaration);
}
```

Both functions use the predefined SyntaxKind. There are much more SyntaxKind but these two definitions are enough for us. In the writing section we will use much more of the SyntaxKind.

2.2.7.   Name of the property

Getting the Name of the Property follows the standard way. You may see that we have to cast to PropertyDeclarationSyntax to get the needed information.

```
public static string GetName(PropertyDeclarationSyntax prop)
{
    return prop.Identifier.Text;
}
```

2.2.8.   GetTypeName

As well as getting the variable GetTypeName type like int or string:

```
public static string GetTypeName(PropertyDeclarationSyntax pd)
{
    return pd.Type.ToString();
}
```

2.2.9.   GetAttibuteList

The attribute handling is last section of the reading part. Doing the same
approach, we are asking for the full attribute list and returning them.

```
public static SyntaxList<AttributeListSyntax> GetAttributeLists(PropertyDeclarationSyntax pd)
{
    return pd.AttributeLists;
}
```

The attributes come in different variations. We can have a single attribute like
keys, required, attributes with additional parameters with text and attributes
with parameters with a kind of enumeration.

This circumstance let us have two functions addressing these cases. Later in the
main program we have to deal with these 2-step approach.

2.2.10.   GetName AttributListSyntax

We overload the GetName function again but this time with the
AttributListSyntax and return the name as string.

```
public static string GetName(AttributeListSyntax item)
{
    return item.Attributes.FirstOrDefault()?.Name.ToFullString();
}
```

2.2.11.   GetAttributParameter

Reading the Parameter returns a string which we can parse later.

```
public static string GetAttributParameter(AttributeListSyntax item)
{
    return item.Attributes.FirstOrDefault()?
        .ArgumentList?.NormalizeWhitespace().ToFullString();
}
```

2.3.   Write the classes (RoslynWriteWrapper)

The second wrapper for Roslyn is our RoslynWriteWrapper; he has all necessary functionality to create a new class. We can create attributes, methods and of course constructors. To remember: it's not a full Roslyn companion and all the functionality is stripped for the ASP developer. If you are missing anything you have the base to add this with a small amount of time.

The writing part is a little bit more complex but will follow a similar scheme as the reading part. Again, this class is also a static class because Roslyn creates every time a new object.

We will use the same standard Model class as in the chapter before, even when we are missing a few pieces like methods and constructors. They will be explained in the text.

```
namespace ASPAutomationTest.Models
{
    //Model Class
    [Table("Person")]
    public partial class Person
    {
        [Key]
        [HiddenInput]
        [Required]
        public int Id { get; set; }
        public string Name { get; set; }
        public string Surname { get; set; }
        [DataType(DataType.Date)]
        public DateTime Birthday { get; set; }
        [DataType(DataType.MultilineText)]
        public string Remarks { get; set; }
        [Display(Name = "From")]
        public virtual CountryOfOrigin CountryOfOrigin { get; set; }
        public int CountryOfOriginId { get; set; }
        public virtual ConnectionStatus ConnectionStatus { get; set; }
        public int ConnectionStatusId { get; set; }
        [DataType(DataType.MultilineText)]
        public string ZweiterRemark { get; set; }
    }
}
```

In the first part we will focus on creating the above class and the needed function for building the class. Additionally, we have to add namespaces and using's but this we will show at the end.

Our goal is that all parameter can easy be creatable strings and then in the wrapper the adaption to the Roslyn syntax will be done.

2.3.1.   CreateClass

Creating the class returns an empty ClassDeclarationSyntax object.

```
public static ClassDeclarationSyntax CreateClass(string name)
{
    return SyntaxFactory.ClassDeclaration(name);
}
```

The result to be clear is an empty class. In this example the name parameter was "Person" and the result after the "CreateClass("Person") operation is:

```
class Person
{

}
```

We have to add everything we need. But this object is the starting point for all operations to build the new e.g. Model class with all the beauties.

2.3.2.   AddStandardClassModifiers

```
public static ClassDeclarationSyntax AddStandardClassModifiers(ClassDeclarationSyntax classNode)
{
    return classNode.AddModifiers(SyntaxFactory.Token(SyntaxKind.PublicKeyword))
        .AddModifiers(SyntaxFactory.Token(SyntaxKind.PartialKeyword));
}
```

In ASP all Model classes must be public and can be partial to add additional code in a different place. We will add both attributes on every class when this function is called.

The result is now:

```
public partial class Person
{

}
```

2.3.3. AddClassAttribute

Classes can have attributes. In our Model class we want to set a specialized
tablename. We are doing this by adding an AttributeList. Even if we have only
one attribute we have to add this as a Attributlist

```
public static ClassDeclarationSyntax AddClassAttribute(ClassDeclarationSyntax classNode,
    string Attributname, string parameter = null)
{
    SeparatedSyntaxList<AttributeSyntax> attributeList = ConvertFlatAttributToList(Attributname, parameter);

    AttributeListSyntax list = SyntaxFactory.AttributeList(attributeList);
    return classNode.AddAttributeLists(list);
}
```

The ConvertFlatAttributToList does this job for us. We have the same behavior
with the properties, so we extract this as an own function to reuse this function
later.

```
private static SeparatedSyntaxList<AttributeSyntax> ConvertFlatAttributToList(string attributname,
    string para)
{
    SeparatedSyntaxList<AttributeSyntax> attributeList = new SeparatedSyntaxList<AttributeSyntax>();
    NameSyntax name = SyntaxFactory.ParseName(attributname);
    if (para == null)
    {
        AttributeSyntax attribute = SyntaxFactory.Attribute(name);
        attributeList = attributeList.Add(attribute);
    }
    else
    {
        AttributeArgumentListSyntax arguments = SyntaxFactory.ParseAttributeArgumentList("(" + para + ")");
        AttributeSyntax attribute = SyntaxFactory.Attribute(name, arguments);
        attributeList = attributeList.Add(attribute);
    }
    return attributeList;
}
```

We have to look after two variants of adding attributes. One attribute with a
parameter like the table attribute with the parameter of the table name plural.
Furthermore the authenticate attribute from a controller which has no additional
parameter.

After calling both methods our class looks like:

```
[Table("Person")]
public partial class Person
{

}
```

2.3.4. AddDerivedClass

Last but not least we have to add derived classes.

```
public static ClassDeclarationSyntax AddDerivedClass(ClassDeclarationSyntax classNode,string name)
{
    return classNode.AddBaseListTypes(SyntaxFactory.SimpleBaseType(SyntaxFactory.ParseTypeName(name)));
}
```

The name of the derived class will be the parameter name. Converting the string will be done in two steps. First the name is parsed and a NameSyntax is returned. The NameSyntax object is the parameter for the AddBaseListType. The result will be shown below.

To add the three classes/interfaces you have to call the function three times.

```
[Table("Person")]
public partial class Person : Baseclass,IInterface1,IInterface2
{

}
```

This is the last function to decorate the class themselves.

2.3.5.   AddClassmembers

To add properties to the class we will use **AddClassmembers**

```
public static ClassDeclarationSyntax AddClassMembers(ClassDeclarationSyntax classNode,
    PropertyDeclarationSyntax propertyDeclaration)
{
    return classNode.AddMembers(propertyDeclaration);
}
```

The parameter PropertyDeclarartionSyntax will be explained in the next chapter, where we build the property from scratch.

2.3.6.   CreateProperty

Adding a property includes a few steps to reach the goal. Here we have two parameters as string. The property type is the variable type like string or int and maybe nullable. The second parameter is the name of the property.

```
public static PropertyDeclarationSyntax CreateProperty(string propertytype, string name)
{
    PropertyDeclarationSyntax propertyDeclaration =
        SyntaxFactory.PropertyDeclaration(SyntaxFactory.ParseTypeName(propertytype), name)
            .AddModifiers(SyntaxFactory.Token(SyntaxKind.PublicKeyword))
            .AddAccessorListAccessors(
                SyntaxFactory.AccessorDeclaration(SyntaxKind.GetAccessorDeclaration)
                .WithSemicolonToken(SyntaxFactory.Token(SyntaxKind.SemicolonToken)),
                SyntaxFactory.AccessorDeclaration(SyntaxKind.SetAccessorDeclaration)
                .WithSemicolonToken(SyntaxFactory.Token(SyntaxKind.SemicolonToken))
    );
    return propertyDeclaration;
}
```

Let's have a closer look at this function. The Property Declaration Constructor takes two arguments: A name syntax which will be created trough the parsing function and the identifier of the property.

The result is an empty property declaration. But having the ASP need in mind we know every property must be public, so we add the public modifier and we have to add the getter and setter.

As example we call this function with PropertyType int and name Id, we will get the result:

```
public int Id
{
    get;
    set;
}
```

2.3.7.   AddPropertyVirtualKeyword

Besides the already added public modifier, sometimes we want to add the virtual modifier.

```
public static PropertyDeclarationSyntax AddPropertyVirtualKeyword(PropertyDeclarationSyntax pd)
{
    return pd.AddModifiers(SyntaxFactory.Token(SyntaxKind.VirtualKeyword));
}
```

The syntax is following the already seen syntax with no additional variations

2.3.8.   AddPropertyAttribute

We are often using additional attributes to control the compilers work, for example the key attribute or datatype attributes.

```
public static PropertyDeclarationSyntax AddPropertyAttribute(PropertyDeclarationSyntax pd,
    string Attributname,
    string parameter = null)
{
    SeparatedSyntaxList<AttributeSyntax> attributeList =
        ConvertFlatAttributToList(Attributname, parameter);
    AttributeListSyntax list = SyntaxFactory.AttributeList(attributeList);
    return pd.AddAttributeLists(list);
}
```

Set the parameter of our PropertyDeclaration, the attribute name and if needed additional parameters for the attribute. The attributes have to be added as list so ConvertFlatAttributetoList will do the job for us. This is the same routine we have already explained above.

2.3.9.   Adding methods to the class (AddMethod)

Adding methods to the class can be a little bit painful. You can create every construct with Roslyn on a step by step basis. For every construct there is a special Roslyn function available. Please refer for the last details to the proper documentation.

We will create standards with ease. This results in that the Roslyn function SyntaxFactory.ParseStatement() will be our primary function we use. The SyntaxFactory.ParseStatement() has one parameter next to others, a string with a line of code. This will be parsed and the return value is a statement value. A statement value can be added to the method. During our long experience with building standards we see this is enough here. We don't have to dig deeper into Roslyn here. If you want to dive deeper into Roslyn please look into your preferred documentation.

We want to abstract everything we needed to easily usable strings.

Our header for the CreateMethod(..) looks like this:

```
public static ClassDeclarationSyntax AddMethod(
    ClassDeclarationSyntax classNode,
    string Methodname,
    string ReturnType,
    List<string> Parameter, List<string> Statements,
    bool AsStatic = false)
```

ClassDeclaration classNode

This is our well known classNode which represent our new class we want to extend with this method.

String MethodName and ReturnType

This is the name of the method and the string for the return type of the function like int or SelectList

List<string> Parameter

The parameter with type and variable name you want to have in this method is like:

"Int a"
"DBSet<Person> dbset"

and so on.

List<string> Statements

This is every line of code in a single string object. Example:

"a +=1;"
"return result;"

Bool AsStatic

When we want to have a static method, we must set the proper keyword.

Putting these things together will result in this source code to extend our class with a method.

```
public static ClassDeclarationSyntax AddMethod(
    ClassDeclarationSyntax classNode,
    string Methodname,
    string ReturnType,
    List<string> Parameter, List<string> Statements,
    bool AsStatic = false)
{
    List<ParameterSyntax> ParameterList = new List<ParameterSyntax>();
    foreach (var item in Parameter)
    {
        ParameterList.Add(SyntaxFactory.Parameter(SyntaxFactory.Identifier(item)));
    }
    List<StatementSyntax> StatementList = new List<StatementSyntax>();
    foreach (var item in Statements)
    {
        StatementList.Add(SyntaxFactory.ParseStatement(item));
    }
    var methodDeclaration = SyntaxFactory
        .MethodDeclaration(SyntaxFactory.ParseTypeName(ReturnType), Methodname)
        .AddModifiers(SyntaxFactory.Token(SyntaxKind.PublicKeyword))
        .AddParameterListParameters(ParameterList.ToArray())
        .WithBody(SyntaxFactory.Block(StatementList.ToArray()));
    if (AsStatic)
        methodDeclaration = methodDeclaration
            .AddModifiers(SyntaxFactory.Token(SyntaxKind.StaticKeyword));
    var _test = methodDeclaration.NormalizeWhitespace().ToFullString();
    return classNode.AddMembers(methodDeclaration);
}
```

Within this function the SyntaxFactory.MethodDeclaration(...) with all the addings create the method and we add this to our classNode.

We love to have a SelectList method with every Model class. This helps us in our views and pages to fill the HTML SelectLists.

In all the example code in Docs and elsewhere this portion of code is inserted directly but we want to abstract from this behavior with this extension.

As always doing some preparation comes first.

We extend the Standards Class with two functions. First GetExtensionclassParameter(string classname) this function will return the used parameter. Putting this into the Standards Class will give you fast access to fit the code to your needs.

```
public static List<string> GetExtensionclassParameter(string classname)
{
    List<string> lp = new List<string>
    {
        $"this DbSet<{classname}> dbset",
        $"object selected = null"
    };
    return lp;
}
```

And the function GetExtensionclassStatments(string idname, string fieldname)

```
public static List<string> GetExtensionclassStatements(string idname, string fieldname)
{
    List<string> st = new List<string>
    {
        $@" SelectList res= new SelectList(dbset.AsNoTracking().OrderBy(x => x.Created),
                        ""{idname}"", ""{fieldname}"", selected);",
        @" return res;"
    };
    return st;
}
```

Now the preparation is done and we can use the CreateExtensionClass() function
to build this extension.

```
private ClassDeclarationSyntax CreateExtensionClass()
{
    var ExtensionClassNode = RoslynWriteWrapper.CreateClass(MF.ClassName + "Extension");
    ExtensionClassNode = ExtensionClassNode.
        AddModifiers(SyntaxFactory.Token(SyntaxKind.StaticKeyword));
    ExtensionClassNode = RoslynWriteWrapper.AddStandardClassModifiers(ExtensionClassNode);
    List<string> Parameter = Standards.GetExtensionclassParameter(MF.ClassName);
    List<string> Statements = Standards.
        GetExtensionclassStatements(MF.Props.GetKey(), MF.Props.ElementAt(1).Name);
    ExtensionClassNode = RoslynWriteWrapper
        .AddMethod(ExtensionClassNode, "SelectList", "SelectList", Parameter, Statements, true);
    return ExtensionClassNode;
}
```

This newly generated class node will be added to the Model file (not shown
here).

The full result of our extension class build looks like:

```
static public partial class PersonExtension
{
    public static SelectList SelectList(this DbSet<Person> dbset, object selected = null)
    {
        SelectList res = new SelectList(dbset.AsNoTracking().OrderBy(x => x.Created),
            "Id", "Beschreibung", selected);
        return res;
    }
}
```

2.3.10.   Add comments

Sometimes you want to add a line of comment to your class or property. You can
do it like adding statements.

We have 2 functions ready for ClassDeclaration and PropertyDeclaration but
keep in mind to add the comment at the last before return the result. If you add
your comment right after a new attribute or something else, the comment can
be on the wrong position.

The parameter of the AddComment(..) function is a string. You can add // but if
the slashes are not present, the function will add them automatically.

```
public static PropertyDeclarationSyntax AddComment(PropertyDeclarationSyntax pd, string comment)
{
    if (!comment.StartsWith(@"//"))
    {
        comment = comment.Insert(0, "//");
    }
    return pd.WithLeadingTrivia(SyntaxFactory.SyntaxTrivia(SyntaxKind.SingleLineCommentTrivia, comment));
}
```

3.   Hub

After we are setting the basics it gets serious. We use the hub and spoke paradigm to build our solution for automation. In the first step we fill the hub class (in the source code ModelFunctionality mf) with all the values entered in the main form. All features we can project has to be implemented in the hub class. Besides the feature opportunities all data has to be loaded in the hub class. There is no and shouldn't be a direct connection between reading the Model class and the Code generation for the different files.

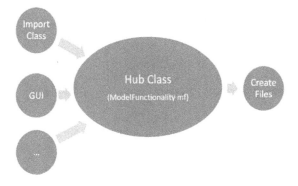

3.1.   Hub class

We create a Hub class with all of our implemented functionality. If you want to have more functionality then you have to extend this class. But keep in mind we want to have a standard where we can have a fast preview of datatypes and usage to show this to our customer and do not repeat every boring step often. We don't want to have an automatic software building tool. To let this be an automatic software building tool the implemented features are not enough and this is not our focus.

Let us have a look into the Model Functionality.

Property	Usage	Remarks
ClassName	The name of the target class	
TableName	The name of the table created by EF Core. The class will be decorated with this entry.	[Table(„TableName")]
AssemblyName	The name of the StandardNamespace. To set the standard Assembly Name for the Models, controller, pages and so on the name will be used to create the right class structure.	<AssemblyName>.Models <AssemblyName>.Controller
AdditionalAttribute and AdditionalAttributeParameter	Both strings will add attributes to the class to decorate the class. Routing parameter can be added using	

	these attributes or anything else.
HasAuthentication	This property will be used to identify that this Model needs authentication. So, it will be used to add the authenticate attribute to the controller.
HasPagination	During the building of the index views or pages this property identifies that the pagination elements should be added. It adds also the code into the controller that pagination can be supported.
Collection of BaseClasses	A Model class can have only one base class, but the base class can have another base class and so on. To have all the properties from the base classes during code generation available, all base classes can and will be loaded. Caution, only the first base class will be written into the Model class

Collection of Interface	Additionally, you can add as much interfaces you want. There are many solutions out there where tagging Model classes with interfaces will call special functions in EF.
Collection of Props	The collection will hold all properties the Model class will have. The details will be explained below.

The hub class is implemented as observable class because we will bind the class to a Windows Forms App. We choose Windows Forms as the easiest solution you can select after a console app. We use the Windows Form only as a container to start, stop and set properties. The Form itself has no active code. If you want to create an own Form in a different environment it should be easy.

We decline the option building this as an ASP Core App himself. Implementing this stateless is much more complicated to understand for you as a reader from our perspective.

The Props are implemented in the PropertyFunctionalityClass.

Property	Usage	Remarks
Name	Name of the property	
DisplayName	In ASP Core you can set the attribute Display Name	[DisplayName(Name = „<DisplayName>")]

IsIdentity	This attribute sets the identity of the Model. It's an extra property to securely ensure the identity. The key annotation might not be enough.	Https://applicationname/classname/Edit/<NameofIsIdentity>

DataAnnotation	The data annotation is an Enum. The following values are already predefined and implemented or prepared to be implemented by you:
	
	`NoOne,`
	`Key,`
	`Currency,`
	`MultilineText,`
	`Url,`
	`Date,`
	`NotMapped,`
	`ConcurrencyCheck,`
	`TimeStamp`
	
	NoOne is the standard. This value creates no data annotation. The other data annotations are following the documentation of EF Core.
		[DataType(DataType.Url)]
		
		Public string website;

VariableType	This Enum stores the possible variable types which are already implemented or prepared. In the Enum the variable types for e.g. string is listed as @string. The reason is that string and so on are already keywords in C#. The Byte Array will be later written as byte_array.
	
	`@string,`
	`@int,`
	`@date,`
	`@datetime,`
	`@decimal,`
	`@ICollection,`	

| | ```
NavigationProperty,
Bitmap,
DateTimeOffset,
DateTime,
@bool,
byte_array
``` | |
	The Navigation Property is used for implementing the 1 to many relationships. The ID Field is created automatically. Sometimes you want to enter the ICollection for the Model. You can do so but it's not needed.	
CSS	During display of the property you can add additional CSS like coloring and so on. Enter here the CSS Name and the CSS value will put it into the view.	
AdditionalAttribute AdditionalAttributeParameter	Attributes like the range aren't implemented but you can use them adding the range into the Additional Attribute and the 0...100 into the parameter property.	[Range, 0..100, Only Values between 0 and 100 are aloud]
IsRequired	This property decorates the Model property with the required attribute	[Required]
IsInIndexView	Yes/no. In the Index view you want not all properties listed. So only the properties having this flag will be shown in the index view	
IsNullable	Yes/no. Stands for himself. If the property must not be	Int?
```

	filled with any value than you can set this property to true.	
IsHidden	Will not be shown in the views or pages but the data will be transmitted to the views	[HiddenInput]
SourceBaseClass	Holds the information to which base class this property belong. If this field is empty than the field belongs to the Model class.	

3.2.   Gui Mode

To fill the data into the hub class we created a Windows Forms where all data fields of the hub class (ModelFunctionalityClass) are bind to the appropriate elements of the form. We decided doing so because this is the easiest way to show the work of this automation without to much complexity from the GUI and necessary file operations.

The ModelFunctionality class and the PropertyFunctionality class are both implementing the INotifyPropertyChanged methods. You are able to bind the class directly to the control. This is what we are doing for all dialogs, lists and so on.

3.2.1.   Main form

Let's have a closer look to the GUI.

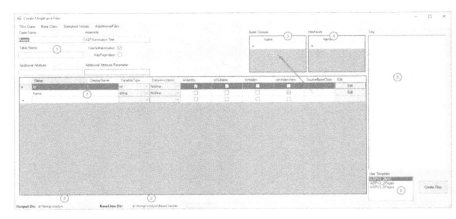

In Section 1 we have the base data for our Model class with Name, assembly and so on. The name for the class and the assembly is prefilled by the standards class. You can change the behavior in this class. All constants and predefined values live here.

The paths in section 2 are as well predefined in the standards class. A double-click on this element opens the Explorer and the content of the selected directory is shown. Into the output directory all files will be written. Understand this as a base directory for your files creation. The class name folder will be created if it not exists under this base path. Below this directory additional files will be written. You can set this during the code generation process. Details will be explained in the "and spoke" chapter.

To operate properly the program must know where to find the base classes to load and parse them. The BaseClass directory holds the paths for the classes.

The green progress bar shows the operation progress during the build process.

Section 3 lists the base classes of your Model. The arrow pointing into the SourceBaseClass field, there the Information is stored to whom of the base classes this property belongs to. You can enter as much base classes you want, you can enter only the first one and then let the program parse the rest of the base classes. Keep in mind that during the write process only the first base class of this list will be written into the Model class.

If you have regular base classes, you can add them into the standards class.
There is a function called with the name

```
internal void InitModelFunctionality(ModelFunctionality modelFunctionality)
{
    modelFunctionality.ClassName = "Person";
    modelFunctionality.AssemblyName = "NorcontractV7";

    var _prop = new PropertyFunctionality
    {
        Name = "Id",
        IsIdentity = true,
        VariableType = Helper.VariableType.@int
    };
    modelFunctionality.Props.Add(_prop);
}
```

InitModelFunctionality. Here you can see the class name and assembly and so on
will be predefined. The BaseClass is from type

```
public ObservableCollection<InheritanceEntry> BaseClasses { get; set; }
    = new ObservableCollection<InheritanceEntry>();
```

and the InheritanceEntry contains only a string.

```
public class InheritanceEntry
{
    public string Name { get; set; }
    public InheritanceEntry()
    {
    }
}
```

The own class is chosen because of the possibility for further enhancements.

Section 4 holds all interfaces. There can be more than one interface and all of
them will be used when creating the Model class. They will not be parsed during
operation.

The class belonging to the interfaces is the same like the base classes.

```
public ObservableCollection<InheritanceEntry> IFace { get; set; }
    = new ObservableCollection<InheritanceEntry>();
```

If you always add interfaces to your Models add them in the standards
InitModelFunctionality function.

Section 5 contains the log where we send information during the process to. The
functionality is implemented using Eventhandlers.

To select the template for a code generation, which one you want to use, is selected in section 6 in the main form. The list box is filled by this function:

```
private void InitializeUseTemplate()
{
    var x = myReflection.GetInheritedInterface("IInterfaceCodeCreationFor");
    listBoxUseTemplate.DataSource = x.Where(t => t[0] == 'I').OrderBy(z => z).ToList();
}
```

Reflection is used to seek all the classes which have the interface "IInterfaceCodeCreationFor" implemented. The results are all classes which have direct or indirect the above interface. Here we are only interested in the interface and with the common name regulation an interface should start with an "I".

The IASP2_2MVC template shown in section 6 is identified by this interface

```
public interface IASP2_2MVC:IInterfaceCodeCreationFor
 {
 }
```

and will be listed in the "Use Template" list box.

The button at number 8 starts the process. The process can be stopped if necessary. All existing files will be overwritten. This is the reason why we do not want to write into the project directory directly. With creating the proper directory structure, we can easily copy them to the target directory in the Visual Studio solution.

The DataGrid (7) contains all property information. The most used features are listed directly in the view. To see all details please use the button "Edit" (9). The details of the property will be explained using the PropertyFunctionality dialog.

3.2.2.   PropertyFunctionalityDetails dialog

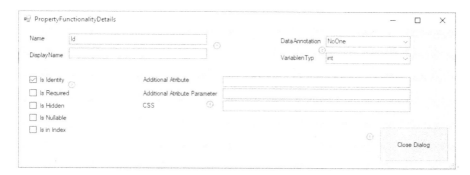

The name (1) of the property stands for itself. It must be valid and will not be
checked for correctness. The display name can be empty. If not it will decorate
the Model property with "[Display(Name = "<DisplayName>")]". It can be used in
the views as well but there is currently nothing special implemented because ASP
is doing his jobs quite good.

Select the type of this property in the VariableType ListBox:

    public enum VariableType

    {

        @string,
        @int,
        @date,
        @datetime,
        @decimal,
        @ICollection,
        NavigationProperty,
        DateTimeOffset,
        DateTime,
        @bool,
        byte_array
    }

The data annotation List Box:

```
public enum DataAnnotationType

{
    NoOne,
    Key,
    Currency,
    MultilineText,
    Url,
    Date,
    NotMapped,
    ConcurrencyCheck,
    TimeStamp
}
```

This data annotation is explained in the docs. All of them should be set only singular. If you have exceptions from this, you have to add them manually later in the source code.

NoOne is adding no data annotation.

But some often used attributes (3) are selectable as Boolean. Is Identity, Required and Hidden creates the corresponding attributes.

Is Nullable adds a question mark to the variable type, from int ID to int? ID.

Is in Index View is an additional features which is used by creating the index view or page. Only the fields having this tag will be added to the table in the index view.

The additional attribute (4) and the corresponding parameter adds the free text attributes to the property. The range is an example for using these additional attributes.

The CSS (4) field allows to enter a special cascade style sheet name to this property. This entry will be added during the creation of the HTML files.

The closing button (5) will store the information.

3.2.3.   Additional features

To make the usage of the program pleasant, we added some additional
functionality which helps in the daily life.

The menu is structured into 4 segments.

"This Class"

Has supplementary functions like import, clear and reset a class even saving and
loading presets.

"Base Class"

Here you load the base classes into the Model or remove them.

"Standard Values"

We implemented the adding of the ModifyUser, ModifiedDate, Create User and
Date in this function. We don't want this in an interface, shadowing and so on.
But If your standards differ remove or change this function.

If you have more standards you want to add to your Model class on demand, you
should think about adding the menu entry here.

"Additional Files"

In our example we use a base controller. To create this for a new project here we
have to create this base controller file. If you use a base page you can add this
here, too.

Let's jump into the details of the functions.

"This Class":

- Import class
  Executing the import class menu let you choose a file by the OpenFile
  dialog. Parsing the class will be later described in detail.
- Clear all Values
  Clears all Values but do not initialize them again. All values will be zero or
  an empty string
- Reset all Values
  Clears all Values and initialize them using the ModelFunctionality.Init
  function.

- Set Base Directory
  To change the base Directory on demand use this function. The new
  result will not be stored permanently, only for this session.
- Set Output Directory
  To change the Output Directory on demand use this function. The new
  result will not be stored permanently, only for this session.
- Save as Preset
  We have often nearly identical Model classes like general settings or
  addresses and so on. To avoid entering the information often you can
  save this as Unicode text.

```
public static bool WritePreset(ModelFunctionality _mf, string path)
{
    string json = JsonConvert.SerializeObject(_mf, Formatting.Indented);
    path += $@"\{_mf.ClassName}.{Program.Standards.ExtensionPreset}";
        File.WriteAllText(path, json);
    return true;
}
```

  The extension can be changed in the standards. The current value is
  ".json".
  Independently during the Create File Process this function is called as
  well. This prevent from entering the same information when the Model is
  changed during the development process. Keep in mind putting
  additional functionality which is not created automatically in a different
  file and add the partial statement.
- Load from Preset
  As expected the reverse functionality is also available. The class is loaded
  using the JsonConvert.Deserialize method. Do not forget to change the
  Assembly.

"Base Class"

- Load base classes
  This function loads all available base classes. Imagine you want to create
  a person class which have as base class AddressBase and this class has
  another base class like tracking and so on. The graphical interpretation of
  this text:

  To have the properties of all base classes in the views or pages available
  the classes must be parsed and the properties have to be added to the

hub class. To identify base classes from the Model, class the source is stored in the SourceBaseClass property.

- Remove base classes
Delete all the fields in the opportunities of the Model and clears the base classes list.

"Standard Values"

- Add Modify Fields
Adding to the list of props the fields Created, CreatedBy, Modified and ModifiedBy. Furthermore, the properties are set to Hidden and String and Datetime.
The RowVersion property for the concurrency will be added as well.

"Additional Files"

Additional Files means that in our newly created ASP Core solution we needed a few files to have them in the solution available like the pagination class or annotation like how to add the Font awesome JavaScript library and other files for different purposes. We follow the same approach as we do for generating code and files for views and pages. We made a folder for "AdditionalFiles" in our solution.

```
▲   AdditionalFiles
    ▷ ⌐ C# AddFile_ViewImport.cs
    ▷ ⌐ C# AddFile_ViewStart.cs
    ▷ ⌐ C# AddFileBaseControllerClass.cs
    ▷ ⌐ C# AddFileIListExtensionToCSV.cs
    ▷ ⌐ C# AddFilePaginationClass.cs
    ▷ ⌐ C# AddFilesToLayout.cs
    ▷ ⌐ C# IAddAdditionalFiles.cs
```

You need to run the menu item "create additional files" in the menu "additional files" once. You get the files for the pagination class, the base controller class and the code for export to csv. The files may vary in the final code.

3.3.   Parse the Model

The second way to get the data into the hub class is importing an existing Model class. You can create a Model class from your database using the appropriate tools or from one of your existing projects.

Select in the main screen "This Class/Import Class" and select the file using the standard file browsing dialog.

In our example we will read a company class with only a few attributes. But this will show you how everything fits together.

The import function runs the following code:

```
_mf.Clear();
var convertModelTo = new ConvertModelToHubClassCSharp(openFileDialog1.FileName,
    Program.Standards.BaseClassesDirectory, _mf);
convertModelTo.DoWorkImport();

modelFunctionalityBindingSource.ResetCurrentItem();
```

_mf is our ModelFunctionality or HubClass. We clear all entries within the current HubClass and create a new ConvertToHubClassCSharp object with a few parameters. We will have a closer look in one minute to this wrapper.

We call the DOWorkImport() function, where the work is done. After the function is returned the HubClass has all the data. We reset the binding source to redraw our dialog.

The company object has the following design:

```
[Table("Companies")]
public partial class Company
{
    [Key]
    public int Id { get; set; }
    [Display(Name = "Name")]
    public string CompanyName { get; set; }
    public string Street { get; set; }
    public string Number { get; set; }
    public string City { get; set; }
    public string TelephoneNumber { get; set; }
    public string WebSite { get; set; }
    [DataType(DataType.MultilineText)]
    public string Remarks { get; set; }
}
```

We see some properties, some properties with attributes, no namespace and no using. In the namespace and using we are not interesting in.

With this explanation in place we have everything to start our import. We call the constructor of the ConvertToHubClassCSharp with the full path of the Company.cs file, the directory where the base classes live and of course our hub class (ModelFunctionality class) the _mf object. The constructor only set the local variables. The DOWorkImport is doing the full job. We want to reuse as much as possible, so the function differs a little bit when we are using the parsing functionality from the menu Load base classes.

3.3.1.   ConvertToHubClassCSharp

The main work of the import is done in this class. We added many comments so you might understand what's going to happen there. But we want to have a closer look as well. The Workflow is easy to follow. We will now take our knowledge put into the RoslyReadWrapper and load all necessary data. The steps are:

1. Load the Model file into memory and convert the file to a classNode
2. Use our RoslynReadWrapper to identify the class name and assembly name from the ClassNode
3. Read the table attribute when it's present
4. Identify and add the base classes using RoslynReadWrapper. Here all bases classes and their corresponding properties will be loaded into the hub class.
5. At least all properties will be identified and added, this happens in ConvertAttributeToPropetyFunctionality and IdentifyVariableType

The last both functions are both most complex functions within the load from a Model file. They must identify attributes like display name or Hidden and so on. But they are straight forward. You may remember that the attributes are hold in a list, so we iterate over the list to catch and assign every attribute. If we haven't any code implemented to handle a specific attribute, in the debug window we get a hint.

Identifying the variable type follows the same rules as the attributes. The only really tricky way is handling the navigation properties. When we read a Model class, we can have xxID and xxNavigationProperty. We only want to have the property once in our PropertyFunctionality list. During the writing we write both properties again. See the Docs for further explanation and the conventions behind.

4.   and Spoke

In the last chapter we filled the hub class with all necessary and possible information. Now we can go ahead and create the code files.

4.1.   Preparation

Before creating the code, here are some last preparation and explanations.

4.1.1.   Folder structure

For an MVC view with controller we need the following files. We organize all files in one folder to easily delete or copy the files when needed.

```
▲  🔲 ASPV2_2MVC
   ▷  ᾰ C# ASP2_2Model.cs
   ▷  ᾰ C# ASP2_2MVC_Create.cs
   ▷  ᾰ C# ASP2_2MVC_Delete.cs
   ▷  ᾰ C# ASP2_2MVC_Edit.cs
   ▷  ᾰ C# ASP2_2MVC_Index.cs
   ▷  ᾰ C# ASP2_2MVCController.cs
   ▷  ᾰ C# IASP2_2MVC.cs
```

You can organize your files as you needed. The files which belong together are identified using the interface later and not to which directory they belong to.

We need the same structure but only for the pages version. You can see much more files but you can create thousands of files if you want.

```
▲  🔲 ASPV2_2Pages
   ▷  ᾰ C# ASPV2_2Pages_CreateCSHTML.cs
   ▷  ᾰ C# ASPV2_2Pages_CreateCSHTML_CS.cs
   ▷  ᾰ C# ASPV2_2Pages_DeleteCSHTML.cs
   ▷  ᾰ C# ASPV2_2Pages_DeleteCSHTML_CS.cs
   ▷  ᾰ C# ASPV2_2Pages_DeleteCSHTML_CS_Roslyn.cs
   ▷  ᾰ C# ASPV2_2Pages_EditCSHTML.cs
   ▷  ᾰ C# ASPV2_2Pages_EditCSHTML_CS.cs
   ▷  ᾰ C# ASPV2_2Pages_IndexCSHTML.cs
   ▷  ᾰ C# ASPV2_2Pages_IndexCSHTML_CS.cs
   ▷  ᾰ C# ASPV2_2PagesModel.cs
   ▷  ᾰ C# IASPV2_2Pages.cs
```

Let's take for a detailed explanation the ASP2_2MVC_Edit.CS File. We see that the class has one base class and 2 interfaces.

```
public class ASPV2_2MVC_Edit : ASPCoreBaseViewsBootstrap4, IASPV2_2MVC, ICodeGeneration
{
```

4.1.2.   Interface IASP2_2MVC

All files you want to create in one step must have the necessary interface implemented. This interface has no code, only the interface himself is interesting. We only want to identify the files using reflection. When all files are found the second interface (ICodeGeneration) come into play. This interface is detailed in the next section.

At the time of writing this book, Asp Core 2.2 was the last version. So, the naming conventions for the MVC controller versions looks like:

>   I -> interface
>   ASP -> ASP, other templates are possible
>   2_2 -> version
>   MVC -> Is for using controllers and views

The pages version will look like:

>   I -> interface
>   ASP -> ASP, other templates are possible
>   2_2 -> version
>   Pages -> Is for using pages

Additionally, you can add your framework like BS4 for Bootstrap 4 and so on.

Keep in mind that this name will be shown in the main form. We think you can work with this proposed naming convention.

4.1.3.   Interface ICodeGeneration

The second interface we have to add to the code generation classes is the ICodeGeneration interface. With adding this interface we can ensure that the CodeGeneration() function is available and in the DoWork() method this function can be called.

4.1.4.   ASPCoreBaseViewBootstrap4, ASPCoreBasePagesBootstrap4

We build all of our files using the standard Bootstrap framework. The same Microsoft is using in the examples and building the TT templates. Bootstrap 4 is the current version at this time of writing, and we create a base class for that. We can see differences how views and pages are handling the same scenarios. This is the reason we overwrite some function of the ASPCoreBaseBootstrap4 class and inherit the specific ASPCoreBaseViewBootstrap4 or the ASPCoreBasePagesBootstrap4. In the specific ASPCoreBaseViewBootstrap4 or ASPCoreBasePagesBootstrap4 we will overwrite the functions which are different.

4.2.   Code creation

The following DoWork() function is part of the worker class and is called from the main form. Here you can see how everything fits together.

We have as parameter a dictionary of string and object where we hand over the OutPut directory, the base class directory, the hub class, the template we want to use and a cancellation token.

```
public void DoWork(CancellationToken ct, Dictionary<string, object> Parameter = null)
{
    SendInfo("Create Class " + Mf.ClassName);
    OutPutDirectory += $@"\{Mf.ClassName}";
    Directory.CreateDirectory(OutPutDirectory);

    var AddAllProperties = new ConvertModelToHubClassCSharp("", (string)Parameter["BaseClassesDir"], Mf);
    AddAllProperties.DoWorkNewClass();

    List<string> ListProcessClasses = myReflection.GetInheritedInterface((string)Parameter["UseTemplate"]);

    foreach (string item in ListProcessClasses)
    {
        if (ct.IsCancellationRequested)
        {
            SendInfo("Cancellation Requested");
            return;
        }
        SendInfo($"File: Create {item} is in progress.");

        ICodeGeneration workitem = (ICodeGeneration)myReflection.InstantiateClass(item);
        ReturnValueCodeGeneration coderesult = workitem.GenerateCode(Mf);

        string OutPutDirClone = OutPutDirectory;
        if (!string.IsNullOrWhiteSpace(coderesult.SubDirectory))
            OutPutDirClone += $@"\{coderesult.SubDirectory}";

        string fullpath = OutPutDirClone + $@"\{coderesult.Filename}";
        Directory.CreateDirectory(OutPutDirClone);
        File.WriteAllText(fullpath, coderesult.Code);
    }
    bool ret = PresetHandling.WritePreset(Mf, OutPutDirectory);
}
```

Let's jump into the code. The checking and tests are not explained further and speak for themselves.

Right after this we create the dictionary with the class name. This prevent to check every time later during the processing for the existence of the directory. Right after the directory portion we have to read all properties from all classes if they are not already loaded. This code is somewhat identical we have seen in the HUB chapter, but we need this again to set all properties correctly for the file creation. Have in mind we need all properties of the class tree available. We must insert all fields, some visible, some hidden, like the timestamp in our views of pages. You can see that we are calling a different function but as said the function is doing the same but has some extra code for checking some circumstances.

With reflection we identify all classes having the interface "IASP2_2MVC" (myReflection.GetInheritedInterface(..) added to the inheritance section of the class. The list of classes should be identical with the files from the directory at the beginning of the chapter, except the interface we ignore this while returning the list of strings. You can create pages files at the same time, or every file you want. The files must have two settings: the template interface and the CodeGeneration interface. There is no limit of code generation with these rules in mind.

After this preparation is done, we can run through the list of files. Checking for cancellation and send the status info.

We use reflection to create an instance of the class. The function behind is Activator.CreateInstance(item) and return this result. Now we have an operational class and we can execute the GenerateCode function. This function will be explained later in this chapter. We will have the ReturnCodeGeneration object, which is explained in the helper section later, but we can see the class in action here. One return value within this structure is the SubDirectory and we create this if it not exists. We have a filename as ReturnValue and of course the code. We will write the code to the text file. We will do this until we have entries which are not processed in the list of files (Variable ListProcessClass).

When everything is done, we will write the preset.

This finalize the full process and you will find all the files at their position and you can copy them into the corresponding directories in your solution. We and a few other developers think the same way, writing to a different directory let you have the control all over the process without changing anything in your project.

4.2.1. Creating the files with Roslyn

All pure CS files could be created with Roslyn, all other file types like CSHtml aren't supported by Roslyn.

That leads us to an interesting question about using Roslyn to build the controller class or the underlying pages class. We have a full implementation of the string operations because we prefer the implementation kind. Nevertheless, we create a Roslyn version of the delete page class and we hope we can support you here. The Roslyn version for the code creation is commented. Please remove comments when needed. All functions are already explained in the Roslyn write chapter and we farm our knowledge now. Keep in mind that we use simple strings that we convert to the correct syntax. If you want to construct everything with pure Roslyn function you may dig deep into this special part of the documentation of Roslyn.

The code generation file is setup in this way:

```
internal class ASPV2_2Pages_DeleteCSHTML_CS_Roslyn : BuildPagesBase, IASPV2_2Pages, ICodeGeneration
{
    Simpleversion|fabmym/en|1futter|Model|ser
    public ReturnValueCodeGeneration GenerateCode(ModelFunctionality mf)
    {
        ReturnValueCodeGeneration rv = new ReturnValueCodeGeneration
        {
            Code = GenerateCodeOfModel(mf),
            Filename = @"Delete_Roslyn.cshtml.cs",
            SubDirectory = @"Pages\" + Standards.GetPluralismenOf(mf.ClassName)
        };
        return rv;
    }
}
```

We want to build pages and so we inherit the BuildPagesPage which often has some useful needed functions.

The interface IASPV2_2 is assigned, so reflection will find the file when this template is in the main form selected.

The ICodeGeneration interface ensure that we have the GenerateCode(..) function implemented. Because the function is called by reflection and will do the work to create the proper source code.

To separate the things a little bit we create in the GenerateCode function only the return value, set the filename and subdirectories if needed. The generation of the code will be done by the GenerateCodeOfModel(..). We hand over the Model functionality to have all the needed values and fields available.

Building a class follows always the same work flow.

```
private string GenerateCodeOfModel(ModelFunctionality mf)
{
    CompilationUnitSyntax syntaxFactory = RoslynWriteWrapper.CreateSyntaxFactory();
    // Add all the Standard using Statement
    foreach (var item in Standards.GetStandardUsings())
    {
        syntaxFactory = RoslynWriteWrapper.AddUsingStatement(syntaxFactory, item);
    }
    // Add the Models to the using statements
    syntaxFactory = RoslynWriteWrapper.AddUsingStatement(syntaxFactory, $"{mf.AssemblyName}.Models");
    // Add the Data to the using statements
    syntaxFactory = RoslynWriteWrapper.AddUsingStatement(syntaxFactory, $"{mf.AssemblyName}.Data");
    NamespaceDeclarationSyntax @namespace = RoslynWriteWrapper
        .CreateNamespace(mf.AssemblyName + ".Pages." + Standards.GetPluralismenOf(mf.ClassName));
    //Create the Class
    ClassDeclarationSyntax PageClassNode = RoslynWriteWrapper.CreateClass("DeleteModel");
    PageClassNode = RoslynWriteWrapper.AddStandardClassModifiers(PageClassNode);
    PageClassNode = RoslynWriteWrapper.AddDerivedClass(PageClassNode, "PageModel");
    PageClassNode = AddStandardProperties(mf, PageClassNode, "Delete");
    PageClassNode = AddStandardConstructor(mf, PageClassNode, "Delete");
    PageClassNode = AddOnGetAsync(mf, PageClassNode, "Delete");
    PageClassNode = AddOnPostAsync(mf, PageClassNode, "Delete");
    // Add the NameSpace and the Class
    @namespace = @namespace.AddMembers(PageClassNode);
    syntaxFactory = syntaxFactory.AddMembers(@namespace);
    //For your convenience and return the Value
    string mycode = syntaxFactory.NormalizeWhitespace().ToFullString();
    return mycode;
}
```

First create the SyntaxFactory, add usings and the namespace. Right after this, create the class himself. To the class you must add the class modifiers. Until here it's standard like building every other class.

From here on we will add the properties, constructor, methods and so on. We listed them one by one in our functions. To every function we hand over the Model functionality for the values and fields, the class we want to extend and which page we want to create. The parameters and method bodies will be different for each of the pages. But we hope this can serve you as a template if you want to extend this generator using the Roslyn version.

For a deeper view on the implementation through Roslyn, we pick the AddOnGetAsync(..) method. The other methods follow the same plan.

```
internal ClassDeclarationSyntax AddOnGetAsync(ModelFunctionality mf,
    ClassDeclarationSyntax classNode, string PagesType)
{
    List<string> Parameter = GetPagesOnGetParameter(mf.ClassName, PagesType);
    List<string> Statements = GetPagesOnGetMethod(mf.ClassName, PagesType);
    classNode = RoslynWriteWrapper
        .AddMethod(classNode, "OnGetAsync", "async Task<IActionResult>", Parameter, Statements);
    return classNode;
}
```

The parameter is the Model functionality and the class node we want to extend. Additionally, we need a control string, to differentiate which page we are currently building.

To feed the RoslynWriteWrapper.AddMethod(..) we need a list of statements and parameters. We build an own function for the statements and parameters so we can recycle e.g. int id, which we need very often.

The GetPagesOnGetParameter(..) is pretty easy. One line of string for every parameter. Surrounded by a if statement to test is the page which should create the delete page. As a hint the create page doesn't need this int id value and of course concurrency should not be an issue as well.

```
internal static List<string> GetPagesOnGetParameter(string className, string pagesType)
{
    List<string> lp = new List<string>();
    if (pagesType == "Delete")
    {
        lp.Add($"int? id");
        lp.Add($"bool? concurrencyError");
    }
    return lp;
}
```

The GetPagesOnGetMethod(..) will return a list of strings for the body. The statements can be on a single line.

```
internal static List<string> GetPagesOnGetMethod(string className, string pagesType)
{
    //After the Statements are parsed by the Roslyn Wrapper, the Source Code is looking shiny again.
    List<string> st = new List<string>();
    if (pagesType == "Delete")
    {
        st.Add($@"if (id == null) return NotFound(); ");
        st.Add($@" {className} = await _context.{className}.AsNoTracking().FirstOrDefaultAsync(m => m.Id == id);");
        st.Add($@"if ({className} == null) return NotFound(); ");
        st.Add($@"if (concurrencyError.GetValueOrDefault())
                    ConcurrencyErrorMessage = {Standards.GetDeleteConcurrencyMessage(className)}; ");
        st.Add("return Page();");
    }
    return st;
}
```

Please be patient you must have one line for every statement. Adding as an example the "Return Page()" to the line before will result in not proper formatted source code.

4.2.2. Creating the files with string operations

Creating the files with string operations is similar using TT/T4 Files. But with one advantage because you can use your favorite editor with full coding support and on the other hand you can avoid learning a new language.

Chapter: Spoke Section: Code creation

Additionally, you can use the string operations for every file and you can take advantages from code reusing all over the place.

Taking the Index.cshtml as an example for building the index view:

The first step is to make the decision if you have pagination available or not. This will result in different Models to use:

```
@model {(mf.HasPagination ? "PaginatedList<" : "IList<")}{mf.AssemblyName}.Models.{modelClassName}{">"}
@{
    ViewData["Title"] = "Index";
}
<h1>List {modelClassName} </h1>
<hr />
```

We use here the PaginatedList from the docs as an example. Now setting the ViewData and the headline of the view.

Secondly, we set a toolbar. We love to have this

```
<div class="container-fluid"><div class="row">
      <div class="col-md-12">
          {GetToolBar("Index", mf)}
```

to allow the customer easily to choose the possible actions like Save, Filter, Search, CSV Export and so on. We show you an example how to do this.

The next step is building the table with the head and body

```
<table class="table table-condensed table-responsive-md table-hover table-bordered table-striped">
<thead class="bg-secondary">
    <tr>
        {CreateTableHeader(mf)}
        <th class="d-print-none"> </th>
    </tr>
</thead>
<tbody>
    @foreach (var item in Model)
    {
        <tr >
            { CreateTableFields(mf, id)}
            <td class="d-print-none" width="75" >
                <a asp-action="Edit" asp-route-id="@item.{id}" class="mb-1"><i class="fas fa-edit"></i></a> |
                <a asp-action="Delete" asp-route-id="@item.{id}" class="mb-1"><i class="fas fa-trash-alt"></i></a>
            </td>
        </tr>
    }
</tbody>
</table>
```

Creating the table header is special implementation, so we created an own function put this function into ASPCoreBaseBootstrap4.

```
internal string CreateTableHeader(ModelFunctionality mf)
{
    string result = "";
    foreach (var item in mf.Props.Where(x => x.IsInIndexView))
    {
        result += CreateTableColumnHeader(mf, item);
    }
    return result;
}
```

In the table header we only want fields we have declared to be there. Normally we want not all fields of the Model in the index view because it will be too wide for all the screens the application will run on.

The CreateTableComlumnHeader(..) function is an abstract function and you can see a few small differences for the views and for the pages.

Back to the header we added a last column for the Edit and Delete menu. But this one should not be printed, and we added the proper CSS style for that.

Building the body is straight forward. The CreateTabeField(..) builds the proper Bootstrap code.

```
<tbody>
    @foreach (var item in Model)
        <tr >
            { CreateTableFields(mf, id)}
            <td class= d-print-none  width= 75  >
                <a asp-action= Edit  asp-route-id= @item.{id}  class= mb-1 ><i class= fas fa-edit ></i></a> |
                <a asp-action= Delete  asp-route-id= @item.{id}  class= mb-1 ><i class= fas fa-trash-alt ></i></a>
            </td>
        </tr>
</tbody>
```

In the last column we added the menu. If you need the details menu, please add this here. We do not use this. In addition, we us Font Awesome to show symbols instead of text but you can also use any font or text like you want.

The result will create this Index page:

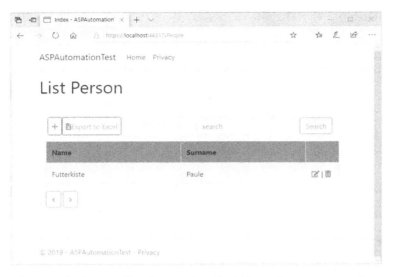

All our standards are well implemented and look identical on every page. The same for Country of Origin:

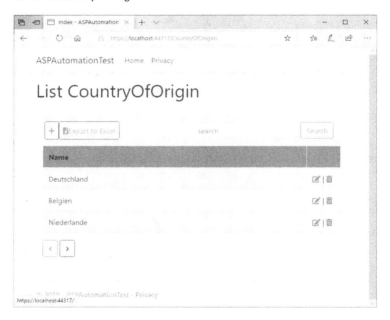

5.   Helper

We use several enums for features and interfaces for identification and last but not least a few classes for supporting the code generation. The following chapters will list every object and explain them in details.

We use reflection to identify the kind of templates to use. Like IASP2_2MVC or IASP2_2PAGES.

5.1.   Helper PageClasses

5.1.1.   ReturnValueCodeGeneration

This class helps to structure the result of the code generation, at the time of writing only three properties are necessary.

Code   Held the generated code from CodeGeneration

Filename   With this name the code will be written to file.

SubDirectory   To structure the code every file can be written into different directories.

                       For the controller you would set this value to controller. For views you would use the class name of the Model.

5.1.2.   Worker

The Worker class is the link between the front end and the code creation. As mentioned earlier in the interface section, the class has three functions. The PrepareWork and FinishedWork stands for them self and you can add additional code as needed. In this implementation they have only small additional value.

The main work will be done in the DoWork class and this function need a little bit more explanation.

For clarity some lines of source code are removed.

```
//Add additional Baseclass Parameter and Attributes
var AddAllProperties = new ParseModelClassCSharp("", (string)Parameter["BaseClassesDir"], _mf);
AddAllProperties.DoWorkNewClass();

//Get all corresponding classes with the Interfacename as Parameter
List<string> ListProcessClasses = myReflection.GetInheritedInterface((string)Parameter["UseTemplate"]);

foreach (string item in ListProcessClasses)
{
    SendInfo($"File: Create {item} is in progress.");
    //Create an instance of the class
    ICodeGeneration workitem = (ICodeGeneration)myReflection.InstantiateClass(item);

    //call the Generate Code from our instantiated class
    ReturnValueCodeGeneration coderesult = workitem.GenerateCode(_mf);

    // Write the code to the file
    string OutPutDirClone = OutPutDirectory;
    string fullpath = OutPutDirClone + $@"\{coderesult.Filename}";
    Directory.CreateDirectory(OutPutDirClone);
    File.writeAllText(fullpath, coderesult.code);
}

// Write Preset
bool _ret = PresetHandling.WritePreset(_mf, OutPutDirectory);
```

The first step is to load all additional attributes and parameters from the base classes. If the parameter from the base class is already loaded the parameter will be ignored and is not loaded twice.

Now we have to find out all possible classes which were marked with the template interface. The "UseTemplate" is the selected template, in our example "IASP2_2MVC". All classes which can generate code for the template search will be searched and get back as list of string. The list should be look "yourclassname_controller", "yourclassname_Edit" and so on.

With this list we now can instantiate the class and call the interface function "GenerateCode". The result of this function will be "ReturnValueCodeGeneration". The return value has all the needed content to write everything to disk.

The last step is writing the configuration of the class to disk. It helps reusing code without copy and paste.

5.2.   Interface classes

5.2.1.   ICodeGeneration

This interface has only one function "GenerateCode". Every class which will create code must implement this interface. Reflection will call this class and execute this function.

```
public interface ICodeGeneration
{
    ReturnValueCodeGeneration GenerateCode(HubClass mf);
}
```

5.2.2.   InterfaceCodeCreationFor

This interface is an only marking interface without any functionality.

```
public interface InterfaceCodeCreationFor
{
}
```

It will be used to mark the templates you have implemented. In our example we have code created for ASP Core 2.2 MVC (IASP2_2MVC).

```
public interface IASP2_2MVC:InterfaceCodeCreationFor
{
}
```

So in the select box in the main form you will see the tagged interface:

Every interface you create and tag with "InterfaceCodeCreationFor" will be shown in this ListBox.

5.2.3.   IWorker

The IWorker interface describes all the possible communication between the front end and the code execution.

```
public interface IWorker
{
    event EventHandler<StringEventArgs> OnErrorOccured;
    event EventHandler<StringEventArgs> OnFunktionFertig;
    event EventHandler<StringEventArgs> OnInformationOccured;
    event EventHandler<StringEventArgs> OnProgressbarAdd;

    void DOWork(CancellationToken ct, Dictionary<string, object> Parameter = null );
    bool FinishedWork(Dictionary<string, object> Parameter = null);
    bool PrepareWork(Dictionary<string, object> Parameter = null);
}
```

In the provided source code the Windows form set all the event handler. They can be set to get additional information during the process.

The DoWork(..) is the working function where the code is generated. The PrepareWork(..) and FinishedWork(..) function is for further usage and do not carry relevant source code.

The parameter dictionary held all necessary information. The cancellation can be provided to see if the user stops the process.

The usage is shown as an example from the main form. When you start the execution of a worker who has the IWorker interface implemented then the parameter must set by you and hand over to the function. When you set the event handler with your code part you will get messages during the process.

```csharp
IWorker worker = new Worker.Worker();
Dictionary<string, object> para = new Dictionary<string, object>
{
    { "HubClass", modelFunctionalityWorkingClass },
    { "OutputDir", OutPutDirectory },
    { "BaseClassesDir", BaseClassDirectory },
    { "TemplateToUse", (string)listBoxUseTemplate.SelectedItem }
};

worker.PrepareWork(para);
worker.OnFunktionFertig -= OnFinished;
worker.OnFunktionFertig += OnFinished;

worker.OnProgressbarAdd -= OnProgressbarAdd;
worker.OnProgressbarAdd += OnProgressbarAdd;

_cancellation = new CancellationTokenSource();
token = _cancellation.Token;

RunningTask = Task.Factory.StartNew(() => worker.DOWork(token, para), token)
```

The DoWork(..) function from the worker will be started in background mode so the GUI will not freeze.

5.3.   Standards class

In this class we bundle all constants with the goal that no string is entered into the code directly.

We hard coded this class, but we know that having a form or a service behind the services could make sense here. But everybody is doing this on his own and we therefor use in this book only the easiest possibly form.

Let us have a look into a few methods to accommodate the ideas and how we used this class.

5.3.1.   Constructor

The class has 4 properties:

- BaseClassesDirectory
- ExtensionPreset
- NameofStartButton
- OutPutDirectory

They are all set in the constructor. Here we hard coded the values for the application. The ExtensionPreset means the extension for the export file of the class. We use json currently.

5.3.2.   InitModelFunctionality()

When you create a new class, this value will be prefilled. Especially the "Id" you might need nearly every time and any other fields you can add here.

We are not adding something like CreatedBy and other values for tracking. They will be added with an additional menu item to have them at the end of entity. Otherwise you can use a base class for tracking and other properties.

5.3.3.   GetStandardUsings()

The standard using's we need within the classes are

- "System",

- "System.Collections.Generic",
- "System.ComponentModel.DataAnnotations",
- "System.ComponentModel.DataAnnotations.Schema",
- "System.Threading.Tasks",
- "System.Text",
- "Microsoft.AspNetCore.Mvc.Rendering",
- "System.Linq",
- "Microsoft.AspNetCore.Mvc",
- "Microsoft.EntityFrameworkCore",

This using's will be returned as list of strings and are very static. If you have own libraries which have to be added regularly, add them here and not in the source code directly.

5.3.4. GetDeleteConcurrencyMessage(string className)

Having the concurrency implemented we have to send the user a notice when this error occurs. When we hand over the class name, we get a more nicely looking message.

The {className} record you attempted to delete was modified by another user after you selected delete. The delete operation was canceled and the current values in the

database have been displayed. If you still want to delete this record click the Delete button again.

This message is taken from the "Docs" and having the parameter inserted. There will be an additional function for Edit, because the text differs a little bit.

5.3.5. GetPageSize()

Even your standards for the paging size can be set here. The value will be entered into the code directly, so if you want to change this value on a specific view or page you can change that otherwise you can ignore thinking about this.

5.3.6. GetPluralismenOf

You may know that the entity designer owns a pluralization service. We use this service to create the pluralization for the directories and so on.

The culture info is set to "en-us". Please change this here if you want to have a different language. And additionally, check if your chosen language is supported.

5.4. ASPCoreBaseBootstrap4

The Bootrap4 classes handle all the code to create the views and pages. This is the only place HTML code is generated.

The class diagram below shows the dependencies from the abstract base class with the derived classes for pages and views. The viewpoint starts from the code generation classes which will build the code and have flagged with the ICodeGeneration interface.

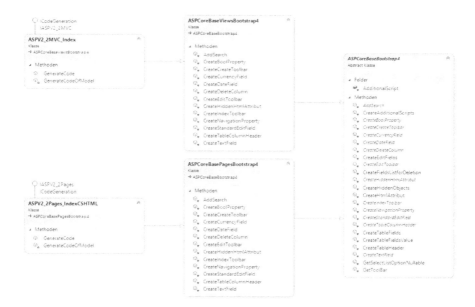

This result for the ASPV2_2MVC_Index class into inheriting the ASPCoreBaseViewsBootstrap4 class and the not shown ICodeGeneration interface and the IASP2_2MVC interface.

One remark: The italic functions are abstract functions.

We prefer building an abstract base class to establish the full needed functionality and build abstract functions when a special implementation is needed. The derived class has to build his own implementation for these functions.

Comparing views and pages you can see that the base class holds only very few lines of HMTL code, the differences between views and pages are really dramatic. This is another reason why we build this solution.

The ASPCoreBaseBootstrap4 class is hold the control mechanisms to build the needed code like we can see here in the CreateEditFields:

We have our hub class as a parameter, and we identify all properties which are not hidden. For every property we have to build the proper HTML code.

```
internal string CreateEditFields(ModelFunctionality mf)
{
    string NewImplementation = "";
    foreach (var item in mf.Props.Where(x => !x.IsHidden))
    {
        NewImplementation += CreateHtmlForEdit(mf, item);
    }
    return NewImplementation;
}
```

The function CreateHTMLForEdit takes as parameter the hub class and the current item. We show the beginning of the function and you can see that we now evaluate the data annotation to call the right code. Currency and the MultilineText has already a special implementation but Url has not. This let the function do a standard fallback when no implementation is provided. For you, you can easily add additional code for an Url. You might want to add a button where the user can click on to open the Url.

```
internal string CreateHtmlForEdit(ModelFunctionality mf, PropertyFunctionality item)
{
    string result;
    switch (item.DataAnnotation)
    {
        case DataAnnotationType.Currency:
            result = CreateCurrencyField(mf, item);
            return result;

        case DataAnnotationType.MultilineText:
            result = CreateTextField(mf, item);
            return result;

        case DataAnnotationType.Url:
            break;
```

The fallback is CreateStandardEditField and is of course an abstract function because views and pages handle this differently. We will have a closer look on this function later in this chapter.

This shows the way we build the HTML code for the views and pages. We explain the possible functions as we do in the chapter before to show you where and how you can jump in.

With the upcoming Bootstrap 5 you can generate a new base class for the ASP Bootstrap content and take fast advantage of the new or changed features. This prevent changing the full code and you have only to adopt the creation of Bootstrap code. You can change this as well for different JavaScript frameworks and even if you use frameworks for the input fields like Kendo or jQuery or anything else.

5.4.1.   CreateAdditionalScripts

When you implement special editors for your fields, like we do for the multiline text field, you may want to add the needed libraries only on this view or page. If you want to do this, you can add your scripts to the local property AdditionalScripts. All the entries will be inserted in the HTML page in the scripts section.

5.4.2.   CreateFieldsFor ... Edit, Delete, IndexTable, ToHide

These functions are the starting point to create the proper HTML code. But before we can create the HTML code, we identify the correct fields. Every identified field will hand over to the creation of the correct HTML attribute creating function.

Using the CreateFieldsForIndexTable function as an example. The properties which belong to the index view are selected and in the order of entered into the properties list transferred to the CreateHTMLForTableFieldsValue function.

```
internal string CreateFieldsForIndexTable(ModelFunctionality mf, string id)
{
    string result = "";
    foreach (var item in mf.Props.Where(x => x.IsInIndexView))
    {
        result += CreateHtmlForTableFieldsValue(item, id);
    }
    return result;
}
```

The other function in this section are following the same pattern.

5.4.3.   CreateHtmlForEdit

Besides the remarks in the beginning of this chapter this function is where the process for the data annotation type is explained. You can also have specific code when the variable type comes into the game.

```
internal string CreateHtmlForEdit(ModelFunctionality mf, PropertyFunctionality item)
{
    string result;
    switch (item.DataAnnotation)[...]

    switch (item.VariableType)
    {
        case VariableType.@bool:
            result = CreateBoolProperty(mf, item);
            return result;
        case VariableType.NavigationProperty:
            result = CreateNavigationProperty(mf, item);
            return result;
        default:
            break;
    }
    result = CreateStandardEditField(mf, item);
    return result;
}
```

For example, Bool values can handle in different ways. You can have true or false as text values for some reasons, but you can also have a checkbox to show the value. The same is valid for the navigation property. Sometimes you want to have a select box in your application, and this is based on the variable. Here you can add more if necessary.

If nothing fit the two switch statements, the standard code for a text box is returned.

The final methods like CreateBoolProperty or CreateStandardEditField are abstract functions. You must implement them in the derived views or pages Bootstrap class.

5.4.4. CreateHtmlForTableFieldsValue

Having the Index view or page in mind we have to fill out the table. Accidently, this is one of the functions with no different implementations for views or pages.

```
internal string CreateHtmlForTableFieldsValue(PropertyFunctionality item, string id)
{
    string result = "";
    if (item.IsHidden) return result;
    result += $@"                    <td class=""{item.CSS}"">@Html.DisplayFor(modelItem => item.{item.Name}) </td>"
        + Environment.NewLine;
    return result;
}
```

We use the standard HTML helper method for displaying the content. Decorate them as table field add if necessary, some special CSS content. Even if we have no extra class attributes, we wrote this attribute to add them easily in the development environment for the target ASP code.

5.4.5. GetSelectListOptionNullable

When you have a navigation property you can have a list where you must select a value. If the field is nullable you don't need to select one. The standard helper can jump in but if the value is nullable it's doesn't work correctly. The result in this function will add the nullable value to the select list.

```
internal object GetSelectListOptionNullable(PropertyFunctionality item)
{
    string result = "";
    if (item.IsNullable)
        result = $@"<option selected>-- Select {item.Name} --</option>";
    return result;
}
```

5.4.6. GetToolBar for index or edit

For the different types of view or pages like index and edit we have different toolbars where you can select from and use them as an example.

The index toolbar looks like:

The plus sign is to add a new entry, the button Export to Excel to create a CSV file or if you want a real MS Excel. On the right side the search box with the Search button.

The edit view or pages has as toolbar

The Go Back sign, the save button and the button to delete the entry.

We use as font "Font Awesome" but Google fonts or anything else can also be used. You have only to ensure that the appropriate files loaded in the views or in the _Layout File.

5.5.   ASPCoreBasePagesBootstrap4 and ASPCoreBaseViewsBootstrap4

Next to our base class for the Bootstrap code creation we have 2 derived classes for the views and the pages implementation. Why do we do this? There are a few reasons to do so.

First one is, most of the current implementations will build on the controller implementation and this is a valid choice at this time. The approach with the pages is new and you might not want to change everything in one step.

Second, the feature set is not identical. We see a few features like globalization where the pages are not fully supporting everything from the controller features. Additionally, a few interesting features are even not implemented yet. This might change over time and this is the reason why we are a little bit diffuse here.

The other perspective is, we can give you more examples to show you variations of implementations. This might help you to find the best way for your personal standard.

As we already now we have a few abstract functions to implement in each of the derived classes.

- string AddSearch(...)
- string CreateBoolProperty(...)
- string CreateCreateToolbar(...)
- string CreateCurrencyField(...)

- string CreateDateField(...)
- string CreateEditToolbar(...)
- string CreateHiddenHtmlAttribut(...)
- string CreateHtmlForDelete(...)
- string CreateHtmlforTableColumnHeader(...)
- string CreateIndexToolbar(...)
- string CreateNavigationProperty(...)
- string CreateStandardEditField(...)
- string CreateMultiLineTextField(...)

For a better reading we removed the parameter which are mostly the hub class and the current property the function has to work on.

At the end every code for HTML has to fit for pages and views. We will give you one example for the CreateStandardEditField function.

The pages implementation:

```
internal override string CreateStandardEditField(ModelFunctionality mf, PropertyFunctionality item)
{
    string result = $@"
    <div class="form-group col-sm-6 col-md-6">
        <label asp-for="{mf.ClassName}.{item.Name}" class="control-label"></label>
        <input asp-for="{mf.ClassName}.{item.Name}" class="form-control" />
        <span asp-validation-for="{mf.ClassName}.{item.Name}" class="text-danger"></span>
    </div>" + Environment.NewLine;
    return result;
}
```

The Views implementation:

```
internal override string CreateStandardEditField(ModelFunctionality mf, PropertyFunctionality item)
{
    string result = $@"
    <div class="form-group col-sm-6 col-md-6">
        <label asp-for="{item.Name}" class="control-label"></label>
        <input asp-for="{item.Name}" class="form-control" />
        <span asp-validation-for="{item.Name}" class="text-danger"></span>
    </div>" + Environment.NewLine;
    return result;
}
```

You can see that the biggest difference is the way the bind data is called. In the pages implementation the property is called through the class identifier. This is similar for all implementations for the Bootstrap code.

This is the reason why we hand over always the hub class and the property. You cannot ensure that the hub class is not needed. This behavior will result in some Visual Studio versions into warning: "CS0168 The variable 'mf' is declared but never used". You can ignore this but during further development and evolution of our standards we might need this hub class.

The rest is easy explained. We take our standard source code for the standard edit file and replace the variable parts with our hub class and needed properties.

5.5.1.   CreateMultiLineTextField

One function we want to point out to show how to implement special JavaScript for another editor. It's an example for every other editor you can choose and there are several frameworks out there where you can choose from.

The particularity of using TinyMCE and another editor is the need to add additional JavaScript code. We have 2 possibilities to add the script code. One is adding the code to the layout file or we can add the script code to the page or View directly.

```
internal override string CreateMultiLineTextField(ModelFunctionality mf, PropertyFunctionality item)
{
    string result = $@"
        <div class="form-group col-sm-12 col-md-12">
            <label asp-for="{item.Name}" class="control-label"></label>
            <textarea id="{item.Name}" asp-for="{item.Name}" class="form-control"></textarea>
            <span asp-validation-for="{item.Name}" class="text-danger"></span>
        </div>
    ";
    string addscript = $@"
        <script src="https://cdn.tiny.cloud/1/no-api-key/tinymce/5/tinymce.min.js"></script>
        <script>
        tinymce.init({
            selector: 'textarea#{item.Name}',
            height: 500,
            plugins: [
                'advlist autolink lists link image charmap print preview anchor',
                'searchreplace visualblocks code fullscreen',
                'insertdatetime media table paste imagetools wordcount'
            ],
            toolbar: 'insertfile undo redo | styleselect | bold italic |
                    alignleft aligncenter alignright alignjustify | bullist numlist outdent indent | link image'
        });
        </script>";
    AdditionalScripts.Add(addscript);
    return result;
}
```

We have two segments in this function.

The first one is returning the plain Bootstrap code to the View or page. All the needed properties are set. When we run this code we will get a text area with in the HTML page.

When you want to use TinyMCE you have to add the JavaScript source code for the editor. The source will load on demand. See the docs for the decision of demand load versus putting this into the layout file.

The next string block is initializing the text area. We use this initializing code for changing the features you will set in the standard here. Do not forget the string "addscript" adding to the AdditionalScripts list. When the page is built all the scripts within this list will be added to the HTML page.

That's all to add a custom editor for a specific variable type or data annotation type.

6.   Add new features

Adding new features to an existing program is always a little bit difficult. We try to support you to prevent tapping in traps. Therefor we show what to do in some common scenarios to extend the software and change existing code.

6.1.   Add a new Bootstrap version

Preparing for a new Bootstrap version has only a few steps. The diagram shows the current hierarchy of the Bootstrap files. You see that every view or page which create HTML code has as base class the proper Bootstrap class implemented. The example shows only the index files but it's the same for every class who create HTML code.

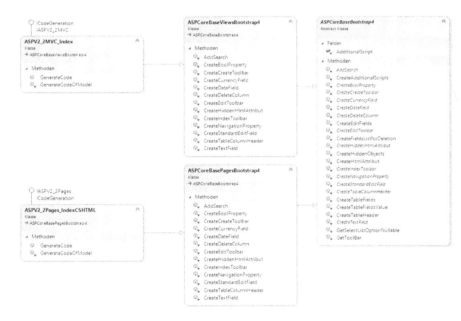

When you do as we do automation for views and pages then you have to create 3 classes. We prefer naming them ASPCoreBaseBootstrap5, ASPCoreViewsBootstrap5 and ASPCorePagesBootstrap5. You need different implementation for views and pages because they are working sometimes differently. Roslyn doesn't come into play because of the lack of support for this type of files.

As we can oversee it now. You need the same abstract and real functions so we would copy all files to new targets and replace the code step by step. When you have done this you set the new base classes to your HTML code generation files.

6.2.   Add or change Bootstrap code only

In our demo code we split everything so you can jump in every piece of the code to change this to your needs. As an example, is creating the edit fields for a particular field.

```
internal string CreateHtmlAttribut(ModelFunctionality mf, PropertyFunctionality item)
{
    string result;
    switch (item.DataAnnotation)
    {
        case DataAnnotationType.Currency:
            result = CreateCurrencyField(mf, item);
            return result;

        case DataAnnotationType.MultilineText:
            result = CreateTextField(mf, item);
            return result;

        case DataAnnotationType.Url:
            break;
```

The CreateHtmlAttribut(..) function calls for every data annotation type a special function. For URL there is nothing special, but you could add code if you want. But multiline text has its own implementation. The code should be in the ASPCoreBaseBootstrap4 class, when looking into the class it's only an abstract function and we have specific implementations for pages and views. Heading to the ASPCoreBaseViewsBootstrap4 file we find the implementation.

```
internal override string CreateTextField(ModelFunctionality mf, PropertyFunctionality item)
{
    string result = $@"
        <div class=""form-group col-sm-12 col-md-12"">
            <label asp-for=""{item.Name}"" class=""control-label""></label>
            <textarea id=""{item.Name}"" asp-for=""{item.Name}"" class=""form-control""></textarea>
            <span asp-validation-for=""{item.Name}"" class=""text-danger""></span>
        </div>
    ";
```

It looks like we expect, and the implementation follows the new guides with ASP-For but we want to add TinyMCE as editor for multiline fields, so we add the needed script. The example shows adding the JavaScript file to this view too. You can of course load the JavaScript file for TinyMCE already in your layout file.

```
<script>
tinymce.init(
        selector: 'textarea#{item.Name}',
        height: 500,
        plugins: [
            'advlist autolink lists link image charmap print preview anchor',
            'searchreplace visualblocks code fullscreen',
            'insertdatetime media table paste imagetools wordcount'
        ],
        toolbar: 'insertfile undo redo | styleselect | bold italic |
                alignleft aligncenter alignright alignjustify | bullist numlist outdent indent | link image'
    );
</script>";
        AdditionalScript.Add(addscript);
```

For this we can add additional scripts to a class and the scripts will be rendered to the view or pages accordingly. With this knowledge you can use every framework to let you show the data in your way you want. Only keep in mind it should be your standard.

6.3.   Add a feature to the Model

Authentication is not a part of the Model functionality. We want to use this as an example to add this. Before we do the implementation, we must look after where the authentication feature will have effect. The new standard for pages is that the authentication flag will be set in the startup and we don't have anything to do. In the controller version we have to add an attribute to the controller with the name Authenticate.

So, we must add a Boolean property to the ModelFunctionality class. In the main form we add a checkbox and set the data bindings to the newly created property HasAuthentication. When we change the state, the data will be automatically set or unset.

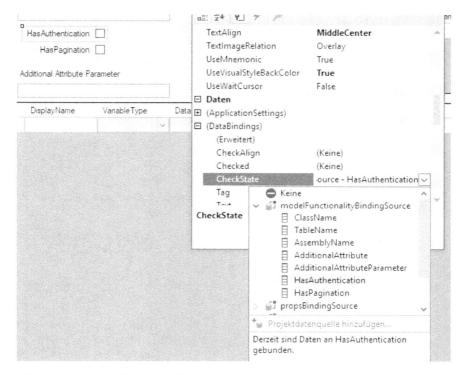

When this is done the front end is finished.

We want to set the authenticate attribute on the controller, so we build a new function.

```
private string ShouldAuthorizeSet(ModelFunctionality mf)
{
    string result = "";

    if (mf.HasAuthentication)
        result = "[Authorize]";
    return result;
}
```

And add a call to the function in the MVC controller generate code.

```
namespace {thenamespace}.Controllers
{
    {ShouldAuthorizeSet(mf)}
    public class {modelClassName}Controller : BaseController
    {
```

If ModelFunctionality.HasAuthentication is set the authorize attribute is returned. This results in setting the authorization attribute on the controller. In generally you can do the same for pages.

6.4.   Add a feature to a property

In the chapter before we have added a new functionality to the hub class. Additionally, we can add new assets to our Model properties. As an example we add a string property

```
public string CSS { get; set; }
```

to the PropertyFunctionality. With this property we can set a special Cascade Style Sheet Value to our property in the HTML code.

In our PropertyFunctionalityDetails page we add a text field and bind this to our newly created CSS property. You can see this in the following screenshot.

Writing HTML code is in the ASPCoreBase(views or pages)Bootstrap4 as you remember. We will add the CSS to the pages file. The same steps are necessary in the views as well.

We want to set this CSS file when the header and fields are written to the HTML file. As an example we choose to show CreateHtmlTableFieldsValue method:

```
internal string CreateHtmlForTableFieldsValue(PropertyFunctionality item, string id)
{
    string result = "";
    if (item.IsHidden) return result;
    result += $@"                    <td class=" {item.CSS} "> @Html.DisplayFor(modelItem => item.{item.Name}) </td>"
        + Environment.NewLine;
    return result;
}
```

to add the CSS to the class.

6.5.   Implement a new version like ASP Core 3.0

The most common expansion of this code is to append a new version of code files, like the upcoming ASP Core 3.0 or implementing an ASP .Net version. The steps are exactly the same.

First create a new folder below your main project node. Name the new folder ASPCore3_0Pages.

Add a new interface to this folder and give the interface the name IASPCoreV3_0Pages. Add the interface IInterfaceCodeCreationFor to the class. Your class should now look like this:

```
public interface IASPV3_0Pages : IInterfaceCodeCreationFor
{
}
```

When you now start the program, you should see in the use template box the newly created template.

When you now hit the "Create Files" button everything is working but no code will be generated because we have no code generation file created.

Let's do this now. Add a new class to folder. Name the class "ASPV3_0Pages_IndexCSHTML". Add the following base classes and interfaces to this file:

": ASPCoreBasePagesBootstrap4, IASPV3_0Pages, ICodeGeneration"

when you append this directly behind the class name, Visual Studio will underline
the interfaces and classes. Use the quick actions to set everything correct. After
doing the quick actions your file should looks like:

```
using Roslyn_ASP_Core_Code_Generation.CodeGenerationBaseClasses;
using Roslyn_ASP_Core_Code_Generation.FeatureFunctionality;
using Roslyn_ASP_Core_Code_Generation.Helper;
using System;
using System.Collections.Generic;
using System.Linq;
using System.Text;
using System.Threading.Tasks;

namespace Roslyn_ASP_Core_Code_Generation.ASPV3_0Pages
{
    class ASPV3_0Pages_IndexCSHTML : ASPCoreBasePagesBootstrap4, IASPV3_0Pages, ICodeGeneration
    {
        public ReturnValueCodeGeneration GenerateCode(ModelFunctionality mf)
        {
            throw new NotImplementedException();
        }
    }
}
```

We encourage you to use the same mythology for code creation as we do. You
can use our template as an example.

For your convenience here are the first lines shown:

```
public ReturnValueCodeGeneration GenerateCode(ModelFunctionality mf)
{
    ReturnValueCodeGeneration rv = new ReturnValueCodeGeneration
    {
        Code = GenerateCodeOfModel(mf),
        Filename = @"Index.cshtml",
        SubDirectory = @"Pages\" + Standards.GetPluralismenOf(mf.ClassName)
    };
    return rv;
}

private string GenerateCodeOfModel(ModelFunctionality mf)
{
    string mycode = "This is my first Code";
    return mycode;
}
```

When you enter this code into your class you will get an Index.cshtml file which
has only Text: "This is my first Code".

Now you are able to extend the code with everything you need and add additional classes for more files.